CLARENCE GAGNON
The *Maria Chapdelaine* Illustrations

Essay by Ian M. Thom

Pomegranate Communications, Inc.
105 SE 18th Ave., Portland, OR 97214
800-227-1428   pomegranate.com
sales@pomegranate.com

To learn about our newest titles and special offers from Pomegranate, please visit pomegranate.com and sign up for our newsletter. For all other queries, see "Contact Us" on our home page.

© 2020 McMichael Canadian Art Collection

The contents of this book are protected by copyright, including all images and all text. This copyrighted material may not be reproduced or transmitted in any form or by any means, electronic or mechanical, including but not limited to photocopying, scanning, recording, or by any information storage or retrieval system, without the express permission in writing of the copyright holders. All rights to the images and text are reserved.

FRONT COVER:
St. Henri de Taillon, 1928/1933
Pastel and/or coloured pencil with graphite,
gouache and watercolour on paper
16 x 23.5 cm (6 5/16 x 9 1/4 in.)
Gift of Colonel R. S. McLaughlin, 1969.4.38

Library of Congress Cataloging-in-Publication Data

Names: Thom, Ian M., writer of added commentary. | Hémon, Louis, 1880-1913. Maria Chapdelaine. Selections. English. | McMichael Canadian Art Collection.
Title: Clarence Gagnon : the Maria Chapdelaine illustrations / essay by Ian M. Thom.
Description: Portland, OR : Pomegranate Communications, Inc., 2020.
Identifiers: LCCN 2019014690 | ISBN 9780764987434 (hardcover : alk. paper)
Subjects: LCSH: Gagnon, Clarence, 1881-1942--Themes, motives. | Hémon, Louis, 1880-1913. Maria Chapdelaine--Illustrations. | Rural conditions in art. | Québec (Province)--In art.
Classification: LCC ND249.G2 C59 2020 | DDC 759.11 [B] --dc23
LC record available at https://lccn.loc.gov/2019014690

Item No. A287
Designed by Stephanie Odeh
Printed in China

34 33 32 31 30 29 28 27 26 25   11 10 9 8 7 6 5 4 3 2

Contents

Acknowledgements	5
Clarence Gagnon's *Maria Chapdelaine* Ian M. Thom	7
The Illustrations	12
About the Author	120

Acknowledgements

I would like to recognize the assistance of the following people at the McMichael Canadian Art Collection: Janine Butler, Alexandra Cousins, Alison Douglas, Sarah Milroy and Linda Morita. This project would have been impossible without your ready help, and it is much appreciated.

Ian M. Thom

Opposite page: *The Chapdelaine Farm* (detail)

CLARENCE GAGNON'S
Maria Chapdelaine

Ian M. Thom

Among the great treasures of the McMichael Canadian Art Collection is a group of fifty-four jewel-like miniatures by artist Clarence Gagnon. Completed in the early 1930s, these are the final paintings made for what is arguably the most famous illustrated book by a Canadian artist: *Maria Chapdelaine*, a novel written by French author Louis Hémon and published in 1933 by Éditions Mornay in Paris. These paintings were gifted to the McMichael in 1969 by Colonel R. S. McLaughlin. Not only were they the first works by a francophone Quebec artist to enter the collection, but they are, for many, the most important.

Louis Hémon travelled to Quebec in 1911 and soon after visited the Saguenay–Lac-Saint-Jean region of the province. The novel, which tells the tragic story of a young farm girl's life, was written quickly after that trip, in the winter of 1912–13. Following Hémon's untimely death in a train accident in 1913, the book was published as a newspaper serial in Paris in 1914. The first illustrated edition of the novel was published two years later, and it has remained in print ever since. It has been illustrated many times—including editions with images by Thoreau MacDonald and Marc-Aurèle de Foy Suzor-Coté—and has been translated into many languages. Indeed, the story has come to so define this region of Quebec that the area is now known as the Maria-Chapdelaine Regional County Municipality.

Clarence Gagnon was born in Montreal in 1881. As a young man he studied drawing in that city, eventually taking classes with painters Edmond Dyonnet, Joseph Saint-Charles and William Brymner. By 1901, he was exhibiting in the annual exhibition of the Art Association of Montreal and working as an artist. In 1904 he went to Paris for the first time, and there he learned the technique of etching. In the years leading up to World War I, Gagnon divided his time between Paris and Quebec, emerging as both a skilled landscape painter and distinguished printmaker. The subject matter of his prints was almost all European, but his painting subjects were predominantly Canadian. Although he achieved great distinction as a painter-etcher in Paris, he retained a deep affection for Quebec, and particularly for the area around Baie-Saint-Paul, the village in which he first settled in 1912. Despite considerable success in Canada (by 1909 he was already an associate member of the Royal Canadian Academy of Arts), he returned to Europe for extended stays, living and working in Paris from 1925 to 1936.

It was at this time that Gagnon turned his attention to book illustration. In 1926, he was invited by the French publisher Éditions Mornay to illustrate Louis-Frédéric Rouquette's novel *Le Grand Silence blanc*. After initially considering woodcuts, Gagnon chose to employ the

Opposite page: *Harvesting* (detail)

technique of monotype for these illustrations. Once he completed multiple preliminary drawings, his process was to paint the image in oils on a piece of linoleum and then transfer it to paper (which had been soaked in oil or petrol), putting both the painted linoleum and paper through a press, under pressure. The resulting images, made using stencils for each colour, were a great success in the book, which was published in 1928. Despite this acclaim, Gagnon had found the problems he experienced in the process—with paper, printers and getting images of sufficient quality—very tiring and discouraging.[1]

Wanting to replicate their success, Éditions Mornay asked Gagnon to illustrate *Maria Chapdelaine*. Following the trials of producing *Le Grand Silence blanc*, Gagnon was initially reluctant to agree. Indeed, he wrote to Eric Brown, National Gallery of Canada director, that he would not illustrate *Maria Chapdelaine* "at any price."[2] Fortunately, Mornay persisted, and a prospectus for subscriptions for the book was published in 1931. It remains unclear precisely when Gagnon began work on the illustrations, though in January 1929 he wrote to Brown that he would "after all illustrate *Maria Chapdelaine*."[3] By December 1930, some fifteen images had already been reproduced by the offset printing process.[4] Thus it appears likely that he was working on the project throughout the period 1929–31, with the printing process continuing until 1933.[5]

Gagnon again employed the monotype technique for some but not all of the works, often augmenting the monotypes with pastel, coloured pencil and other drawing media. As he had done for *Le Grand Silence blanc*, Gagnon made numerous preliminary studies for many of the *Maria Chapdelaine* works, the final paintings being among his highest achievements. Although the process of producing the book exhausted Gagnon, his perfectionism and attention to detail ensured that *Maria Chapdelaine* remains one the most beautiful illustrated books ever produced by a Canadian artist. It was also Gagnon's last illustration project.

Gagnon's approach to Hémon's narrative was quite different from that taken by previous illustrators. He had

Portrait of Clarence Gagnon, n.d.
City of Montreal Archives, BM83_2P22

never been to the Saguenay–Lac-Saint-Jean region of Quebec and therefore relied on his memories of Baie-Saint-Paul and the surrounding Charlevoix landscape as the setting for the narrative. While the story has several strong characters, Gagnon chose not to concentrate on them but rather to evoke the lifestyle of the countryside he so loved. We see the passing of the seasons, the work of the people and the cycle of life and death. The central story of Hémon's novel—the choices that Maria Chapdelaine has to make about her life, whom to marry, where to live and so on—are, for the most part, not alluded to specifically, and yet the images are powerfully evocative. As scholars Hélène Sicotte and Michèle Grandbois have noted, it is "a story shaped by memory"—Gagnon's memory.[6]

How vivid those memories are! *The Last Crossing* (p. 23), showing a driver, horse and sleigh dashing across the ice as it cracks, is spirited and conveys the frisson of danger. *François Paradis Camping in the Snow* (p. 37) suggests how small each of us is in the vastness of nature. The importance of church and of community are revealed in images such as *Leaving Church* (p. 15), *Christmas Mass* (p. 77) and *Napoléon Laliberté Reports Village News* (p. 19). The harsh conditions of these lives in the country emerge in *Logging Camp Near Vermillion* (p. 83), *Fetching Water* (p. 99) and *Burning Stumps* (p. 45). Landscapes such as *Northern Land* (p. 13), *Thunder of the Rapids* (p. 33), *Early July* (p. 49) and *Hills at Dusk* (p. 97) reveal the majesty of the terrain.

The care that Gagnon took in creating these images is exceptional. Each composition is a complete statement despite its diminutive size. *Village Life* (p. 27), which shows young girls being led to their First Communion along a wooden boardwalk through the village, is a masterpiece of light and shade. The foreground of the image is in shadow and the background in brilliant sunshine. The gentle meander of the boardwalk leads the eye into the composition, and the contrast between the young communicant in the foreground and her widowed grandmother—black and white—is delicately handled. *Spring Mud* (p. 93), in which a man and horse are depicted struggling to get a wagon up a hill, introduces a palpable sense of movement through the straining horse and the curve of wagon, both of which lead the eye and mind to urge their journey onward. In *Eutrope Gagnon Visits* (p. 31), three different sources of light are handled magnificently: from the lantern, from the windows of the house and from the stars in the sky. Another wonderful touch is the subtle suggestion that Eutrope is wearing a plaid coat. Even though we do not see his face, we get a sense, through the positioning of his body, that this visit is one of both determination and trepidation as he advances his suit for Maria's hand. *The Day After the Storm* (p. 79) conveys the sheer labour of these men bundled against the cold.

A telling example of Gagnon's attention to detail is the distinctive colour of the snow where it has been shovelled or plowed. *Christmas Mass* (p. 77) vividly conveys both the bitter weather (in the wisps of snow sweeping off the church roof and the swept-up scarf of the woman in the foreground) and the central importance of the church and spiritual life in the community, evoked by the warm shaft of light that floods from the open church door. Another fascinating image is *Killing the Pig* (p. 73). While Gagnon does not depict the facial expressions in detail, we get a clear sense of the effort the three adults expend make sure nothing from the pig is wasted, as well as the curiosity of the little boy and his dog who look on, and the boredom of the little girl no longer being pulled on her sleigh. Again and again, Gagnon provides small, telling details in these works that give them a sense of authenticity, even though we know these were not events that he had experienced firsthand. Look, for example, at *The Great Drive* (p. 51), where the perilous stance of the man in the left foreground, and the telling curvature of his pike, strongly suggest his straining effort. Gagnon's images are far more than illustrations. They conjure a world. As Sicotte and Grandbois have written, they are "Gagnon's testament . . . his whole career is in a sense condensed into this final major project."[7]

Gagnon realized how important these works were and wanted them to remain together. In 1938, they were exhibited in Ottawa, Toronto and Montreal to great acclaim. One reviewer wrote:

> They were notable for the richness of their color, the exquisite spirit of their mood and the remarkable texture that the artist obtained. No series of illustrations half as good had ever been created by a Canadian artist and few by a European or United States artist.[8]

In 1939, Gagnon was asked to lend some of the works to Rideau Hall to decorate the rooms being used by King George VI and Queen Elizabeth.[9] Following the royal tour, the illustrations were returned to Gagnon, and they remained in his possession until his death. Gagnon's widow, Lucile Rodier Gagnon, arranged to sell the whole group to Colonel R. S. McLaughlin with the understanding that the ensemble would never be split up.[10] McLaughlin, one of the founders of General Motors in Canada, installed these works and those of other artists in his home, Parkwood Estate, in Oshawa, Ontario. McLaughlin was an important collector and had many now iconic works in his home. In time, he would become an extremely significant donor to the McMichael, giving major works by many artists.[11] The *Maria Chapdelaine* illustrations, however, were in a category of their own. Robert McMichael vividly described his first encounter with these works in the company of Colonel McLaughlin's daughter, artist Isabel McLaughlin:

> Isabel led us up the great staircase to a large sitting room next to her father's bedroom suite and we sensed by her excitement that this room was to be the climax of our tour. The entire area was carpeted and decorated in muted greys, a perfect setting for the scores of small paintings in equal-sized frames which surrounded us. It was a major art collection within a collection—the fifty-four magnificent illustrations which had been created by the great Quebec artist, Clarence Gagnon, for the famous 1933 Mornay Édition of Louis Hémon's classic French-Canadian novel, *Maria Chapdelaine*.[12]

The gift of Gagnon's *Maria Chapdelaine* illustrations by Colonel McLaughlin immediately enriched the McMichael Canadian Art Collection with perhaps the most significant group of Gagnon works in existence.

Gagnon began his career by achieving enormous success as a painter-etcher, but by the end of World War I he had largely abandoned printmaking for painting. His love of Canada continued to animate his work, even though many of the paintings were produced in Paris. His career as an illustrator was short: he produced illustrations for only two books, but they are both remarkable.[13] Of the two, only the illustrations for *Maria Chapdelaine* have remained as a complete group, as was Gagnon's wish.

Gagnon remained in Paris until late 1936, when he returned to Canada permanently. His painting days were over, though he devoted himself to a variety of projects, lecturing, serving on boards and trying to establish an open-air museum on the Île d'Orléans. Gagnon doubtless realized that, in the *Maria Chapdelaine* illustrations, he had completed his *chef-d'oeuvre*. Following surgery for pancreatic cancer, Gagnon died in January 1942, leaving a timeless and truly remarkable legacy and a profound document of the life and people of Quebec.

Notes

1 Hélène Sicotte and Michèle Grandbois, *Clarence Gagnon, 1881–1942: Dreaming the Landscape* (Quebec: Musée national des beaux-arts du Québec and Les Éditions de L'Homme, 2006), 184.

2 Gagnon to Eric Brown, March 14, 1928, NGC Fonds, National Gallery of Canada Library and Archives, Box 259, File 14.

3 Gagnon to Eric Brown, January 11, 1929, NGC Fonds, National Gallery of Canada Library and Archives, Box 259, File 14.

4 Sicotte and Grandbois, *Clarence Gagnon*, 198.

5 For a detailed outline of the process, see Sicotte and Grandbois, *Clarence Gagnon*, 198–201.

6 Sicotte and Grandbois, *Clarence Gagnon*, 201.

7 Sicotte and Grandbois, *Clarence Gagnon*, 206.

8 E. W. Hammond, "C. Gagnon's Illustrations for 'Maria Chapdelaine' Now at National Gallery," *Ottawa Citizen*, March 11, 1938.

9 Kenneth G. Wright, "Clarence Gagnon to Receive Honor," *Montreal Gazette*, January 2, 1939.

10 Robert McMichael, *One Man's Obsession* (Scarborough, ON: Prentice-Hall Canada, 1986), 235.

11 In addition to the Gagnon illustrations, Colonel McLaughlin donated thirty works by the following artists: Franklin Carmichael, Emily Carr, A. J. Casson, Maurice Cullen, Lawren S. Harris, A. Y. Jackson, Arthur Lismer, J. E. H. MacDonald, Isabel McLaughlin, J. W. Morrice, A. H. Robinson, Tom Thomson and Frederick Varley.

12 McMichael, *One Man's Obsession*, 234–35.

13 A third book, W. H. Blake's *Brown Waters*, published in 1940, uses Gagnon images as illustrations, but Gagnon did not produce paintings specifically for it.

The Illustrations

The text excerpts included herein are from the 1921 translation by W. H. Blake of Louis Hémon's *Maria Chapdelaine* (Toronto: Macmillan Co. of Canada, 1921). These extended excerpts have been identified using the original pairings between text and images presented by Clarence Gagnon in the *Catalogue of the Exhibition of Fifty-Four Original Paintings by Clarence Gagnon, Illustrating the Book "Maria Chapdelaine,"* published by the Art Association of Montreal in 1938.

Northern Land, 1928/1933. Gouache and mixed media on paper, 7.3 x 7.9 cm (2⁷⁄₈ x 3⅛ in.). Gift of Colonel R. S. McLaughlin, 1969.4.1

CLARENCE GAGNON | The *Maria Chapdelaine* Illustrations

The door opened, and the men of the congregation began to come out of the church at Péribonka.

—*Maria Chapdelaine*, page 11

Leaving Church, 1928/1933
Watercolour, gouache and pastel
over graphite on paper
20.8 x 21.4 cm (8³⁄₁₆ x 8⁷⁄₁₆ in.)
Gift of Colonel R. S. McLaughlin, 1969.4.4

CLARENCE GAGNON | The *Maria Chapdelaine* Illustrations

This chill and universal white, the humbleness of the wooden church and the wooden houses scattered along the road, the gloomy forest edging so close that it seemed to threaten, these all spoke of a harsh existence in a stern land.

—*Maria Chapdelaine*, page 11

Church at Peribonka, 1928/1933
Gouache and watercolour on paper
15.5 x 22.6 cm (6⅛ x 8⅞ in.)
Gift of Colonel R. S. McLaughlin, 1969.4.2

CLARENCE GAGNON | The *Maria Chapdelaine* Illustrations

At length the talk slackened and all faced the top step, where Napoléon Laliberté was making ready, in accord with his weekly custom, to announce the parish news.

—*Maria Chapdelaine*, page 14

Napoléon Laliberté Reports Village News, 1928/1933
Gouache and pastel with watercolour on paper
17.3 x 21.8 cm (6 13/16 x 8 9/16 in.)
Gift of Colonel R. S. McLaughlin, 1969.4.3

CLARENCE GAGNON | The *Maria Chapdelaine* Illustrations

Driving always made him sleepy, and the horse, aware that the usual drowsiness had possession of his master, slackened his pace and at length fell to a walk.

—*Maria Chapdelaine*, page 27

Sleeping on the Way Home, 1928/1933
Watercolour and gouache over graphite on paper
18.5 x 19.1 cm (7⁵⁄₁₆ x 7½ in.)
Gift of Colonel R. S. McLaughlin, 1969.4.5

CLARENCE GAGNON | The *Maria Chapdelaine* Illustrations

Old Chapdelaine, fully awake now, was on his feet; his eyes beneath the fur cap shone with courage and quick resolve. . . .

    Just as they reached land a cake of ice tilted beneath their weight and sank, leaving a space of open water.

—*Maria Chapdelaine*, page 33

The Last Crossing, 1928/1933
Watercolour, gouache and mixed media on paper
18.6 x 17.9 cm (7 5/16 x 7 1/16 in.)
Gift of Colonel R. S. McLaughlin, 1969.4.6

CLARENCE GAGNON | The *Maria Chapdelaine* Illustrations

Soon the travellers discerned a clearing in the forest, a mounting column of smoke, the bark of a dog.

"They will be glad to see you again, Maria," said her father. "They have been lonesome for you, every one of them."

—*Maria Chapdelaine*, page 34

The Chapdelaine Farm, 1928/1933
Watercolour and gouache with pastel
or coloured pencil (?) on paper
16.4 x 22.2 cm (6⁷⁄₁₆ x 8¾ in.)
Gift of Colonel R. S. McLaughlin, 1969.4.7

CLARENCE GAGNON | The *Maria Chapdelaine* Illustrations

Madame Chapdelaine stirred the fire in the big cast-iron stove, came and went, brought from the cupboard plates and dishes, the loaf of bread and pitcher of milk, tilted the great molasses jar over a glass jug. Not seldom she stopped to ask Maria something, or to catch what she was saying, and stood for a few moments dreaming, hands on her hips, as the villages spoken of rose before her in memory.

—*Maria Chapdelaine*, pages 35–36

Village Life, 1928/1933
Gouache with watercolour and
coloured pencil on paper
20.1 x 22.6 cm (7¹⁵⁄₁₆ x 8⅞ in.)
Gift of Colonel R. S. McLaughlin, 1969.4.8

CLARENCE GAGNON | The *Maria Chapdelaine* Illustrations

To Maria it was as though since her absence, she was giving attention for the first time in her life to these sounds and movements; that they possessed a different significance from movements and sounds elsewhere, and invested with some peculiar quality of sweetness and peace all that happened in that house far off in the woods.

—*Maria Chapdelaine*, page 41

Baking and Weaving, 1928/1933
Coloured pencil and/or pastel, with gouache
and Conté crayon on paper
22.1 x 23.4 cm (8 11/16 x 9 3/16 in.)
Gift of Colonel R. S. McLaughlin, 1969.4.9

CLARENCE GAGNON | The *Maria Chapdelaine* Illustrations

"A visitor," announced Mother Chapdelaine, "Eutrope Gagnon has come over to see us."

It was an easy guess, as Eutrope Gagnon was their only neighbour.... He appeared on the threshold, lantern in hand.

—*Maria Chapdelaine*, pages 41–42

Eutrope Gagnon Visits, 1928/1933
Pastel and coloured pencil with gouache on paper
18.7 x 18.6 cm (7⅜ x 7⁵⁄₁₆ in.)
Gift of Colonel R. S. McLaughlin, 1969.4.10

CLARENCE GAGNON | The *Maria Chapdelaine* Illustrations

One morning three days later, on opening the door, Maria's ear caught a sound that made her stand motionless and listening. The distant and continuous thunder was the voice of wild waters, silenced all winter by the frost.

—*Maria Chapdelaine*, page 51

Thunder of the Rapids, 1928/1933
Gouache over colour monotype on paper
17.9 x 24.1 cm (7 1/16 x 9 1/2 in.)
Gift of Colonel R. S. McLaughlin, 1969.4.11

Replying to further questions he spoke of his journeys on the North Shore and to the head-waters of the rivers—of it all very naturally and with a shade of hesitation, scarcely knowing what to tell and what to leave out, for the people he was speaking to lived in much the same kind of country and their manner of life was little different.

—*Maria Chapdelaine*, page 57

François Paradis in the North, 1928/1933
Watercolour and coloured pencil and/or
pastel with gouache on paper
20.2 x 18.2 cm (7$^{15}/_{16}$ x 7$^{3}/_{16}$ in.)
Gift of Colonel R. S. McLaughlin, 1969.4.13

CLARENCE GAGNON | The *Maria Chapdelaine* Illustrations

"Up there the winters are harder yet than here, and still longer. We have only dogs to draw our sleds, fine strong dogs, but bad-tempered and often half wild."

—*Maria Chapdelaine*, page 57

François Paradis Camping in the Snow, 1928/1933
Gouache with watercolour and coloured
pencil and/or pastel on paper
18.3 x 22 cm (7³⁄₁₆ x 8¹¹⁄₁₆ in.)
Gift of Colonel R. S. McLaughlin, 1969.4.12

CLARENCE GAGNON | The *Maria Chapdelaine* Illustrations

Scarcely was François gone when the two women and Tit'Bé knelt for the evening prayer. The mother led in a high voice, speaking very rapidly, the others answering in a low murmur.

—*Maria Chapdelaine*, page 60

Evening Prayer, 1928/1933
Coloured pencil and/or pastel,
with watercolour on paper
19.7 x 20.9 cm (7¾ x 8¼ in.)
Gift of Colonel R. S. McLaughlin, 1969.4.14

CLARENCE GAGNON | The *Maria Chapdelaine* Illustrations

After a few chilly days, June suddenly brought veritable spring weather. A blazing sun warmed field and forest, the lingering patches of snow vanished even in the deep shade of the woods; the Péribonka rose and rose between its rocky banks until the alders and the roots of the nearer spruces were drowned; in the roads the mud was incredibly deep.

—*Maria Chapdelaine*, page 62

Spring Arrives, 1928/1933
Gouache with watercolour and coloured pencil and/or pastel on paper
16.1 x 22.9 cm (6⁵⁄₁₆ x 9 in.)
Gift of Colonel R. S. McLaughlin, 1969.4.15

CLARENCE GAGNON | The *Maria Chapdelaine* Illustrations

The place where they had worked in the morning was still full of stumps and overgrown with alders. They set themselves to cutting and uprooting the alders, gathering a sheaf of branches in the hand and severing them with the ax, or sometimes digging the earth away about the roots and tearing up the whole bush together. The alders disposed of, there remained the stumps.

    Légaré and Esdras attacked the smaller ones with no weapons but their axes and stout wooden prizes.

—*Maria Chapdelaine*, pages 69–70

Making Land, 1928/1933
Watercolour and gouache over Conté crayon
with coloured pencil and/or pastel on paper
20.1 x 22 cm (7$^{15}/_{16}$ x 8$^{11}/_{16}$ in.)
Gift of Colonel R. S. McLaughlin, 1969.4.16

CLARENCE GAGNON | The *Maria Chapdelaine* Illustrations

They first cut the roots spreading on the surface, then drove a lever well home, and, chests against the bar, threw all their weight upon it.

—*Maria Chapdelaine*, page 70

Burning Stumps, 1928/1933
Gouache over Conté crayon with coloured
pencil and/or pastel on paper
20.6 x 20.9 cm (8⅛ x 8¼ in.)
Gift of Colonel R. S. McLaughlin, 1969.4.18

CLARENCE GAGNON | The *Maria Chapdelaine* Illustrations

The sun dipped toward the horizon, disappeared; the sky took on softer hues above the forest's dark edge, and the hour of supper brought to the house five men of the colour of the soil.

—*Maria Chapdelaine*, page 71

Day's End, 1928/1933
Watercolour with coloured pencil
and/or pastel on paper
21.2 x 21.7 cm (8⅜ x 8⁹⁄₁₆ in.)
Gift of Colonel R. S. McLaughlin, 1969.4.17

CLARENCE GAGNON | The *Maria Chapdelaine* Illustrations

The fine weather continued, and early in July the blueberries were ripe.

—*Maria Chapdelaine*, page 77

Early July, 1928/1933
Gouache with coloured pencil and graphite
over colour monotype on paper
15.9 x 23 cm (6¼ x 9¹/₁₆ in.)
Gift of Colonel R. S. McLaughlin, 1969.4.19

CLARENCE GAGNON | The *Maria Chapdelaine* Illustrations

At every abrupt turn, at every fall, where logs jam and pile, must be found the strong and nimble river-drivers, practised at the dangerous work, at making their way across the floating timber, breaking the jams, aiding with ax and pike-pole the free descent of this moving forest.

—*Maria Chapdelaine*, page 80

The Great Drive, 1928/1933
Pastel and/or coloured pencil, gouache and
watercolour over graphite (?) on paper
20.8 x 21.2 cm (8 3/16 x 8 3/8 in.)
Gift of Colonel R. S. McLaughlin, 1969.4.20

CLARENCE GAGNON | The *Maria Chapdelaine* Illustrations

The party ran its quiet course. An hour of cards, some talk with a visitor who bears news from the great world, these are still accounted happiness in the Province of Quebec.

—*Maria Chapdelaine*, page 93

Exchanging Stories, 1928/1933
Oil pastel with gouache over Conté crayon on paper
21.8 x 23.2 cm (8 9/16 x 9 1/8 in.)
Gift of Colonel R. S. McLaughlin, 1969.4.21

CLARENCE GAGNON | The *Maria Chapdelaine* Illustrations

The blueberries were fully ripe. In the burnt lands the purple of the clusters and the green of the leaves now overcame the paling rose of the laurels. The children began picking at once with cries of delight, but their elders scattered through the woods in search of the larger patches, where one might sit on one's heels and fill a pail in an hour.

—*Maria Chapdelaine*, page 96

Picking Blueberries, 1928/1933
Pastel and/or coloured pencil with charcoal on paper
17.9 x 20.1 cm (7 1/16 x 7 15/16 in.)
Gift of Colonel R. S. McLaughlin, 1969.4.22

CLARENCE GAGNON | The *Maria Chapdelaine* Illustrations

But next day the wind had backed afresh, and the cheerful clouds of yesterday, now torn and shapeless, straggling in disorderly rout, seemed to be fleeing like the wreckage of a broken army. . . .

Yet the Power at length was pleased to show indulgence, and the north-west wind blew for three days on end, steady and strong, promising a rainless week.

—*Maria Chapdelaine*, pages 102–103

The White Horse, 1928/1933
Watercolour and gouache over graphite with pastel and/or coloured pencil on paper
15.7 x 21.5 cm (6 3/16 x 8 7/16 in.)
Gift of Colonel R. S. McLaughlin, 1969.4.23

CLARENCE GAGNON | The *Maria Chapdelaine* Illustrations

Flies and mosquitos rose in swarms from the cut hay, stinging and tormenting the workers; a blazing sun scorched their necks, and smarting sweat ran into their eyes; when evening came, such was the ache of backs continually bent, they could not straighten themselves without making wry faces.

—*Maria Chapdelaine,* page 104

Haying, 1928/1933
Pastel and/or coloured pencil with
gouache and graphite on paper
19.2 x 20.7 cm (7 9/16 x 8 1/8 in.)
Gift of Colonel R. S. McLaughlin, 1969.4.24

CLARENCE GAGNON | The *Maria Chapdelaine* Illustrations

Twenty paces from the house the clay oven with its sheltering roof of boards loomed dark, but the door of the fireplace fitted badly and one red gleam escaped through the chink; the dusky border of the forest stole a little closer in the night. Maria sat very still, delighting in the quiet and the coolness, while a thousand vague dreams circled about her like a flock of wheeling birds.

—*Maria Chapdelaine*, page 108

Maria Daydreams, 1928/1933
Gouache with coloured pencil over
colour monotype on paper
19.5 x 20.4 cm (7¹¹⁄₁₆ x 8¹⁄₁₆ in.)
Gift of Colonel R. S. McLaughlin, 1969.4.25

CLARENCE GAGNON | The *Maria Chapdelaine* Illustrations

September arrived, and the dryness so welcome for the haymaking persisted till it became a disaster. According to the Chapdelaines, never had the country been visited with such a drought as this, and every day a fresh motive was suggested for the divine displeasure.

—*Maria Chapdelaine*, page 114

September Arrives, 1928/1933
Gouache with watercolour over graphite on paper
16.8 x 23.7 cm (6⅝ x 9⁵⁄₁₆ in.)
Gift of Colonel R. S. McLaughlin, 1969.4.26

CLARENCE GAGNON | The *Maria Chapdelaine* Illustrations

Through the increasing cold, the early frosts, the threats of snow, they held back their hands and put off the reaping from day to day, encouraging the meagre grain to steal a little nourishment from the earth's failing veins and the spiritless sun. At length, harvest they must, for October approached. About the time when the leaves of birches and aspens were turning, the oats and the wheat were cut and carried to the barn under a cloudless sky, but without rejoicing.

—*Maria Chapdelaine*, page 116

Harvesting, 1928/1933
Gouache over graphite with pastel and/or
coloured pencil and watercolour on paper
21.4 x 19.1 cm (8 7/16 x 7 1/2 in.)
Gift of Colonel R. S. McLaughlin, 1969.4.27

CLARENCE GAGNON | The *Maria Chapdelaine* Illustrations

One October morning Maria's first vision on arising was of countless snow-flakes sifting lazily from the skies. The ground was covered, the trees white; verily it seemed that autumn was over, when in other lands it had scarce begun.

—*Maria Chapdelaine*, page 118

The First Snow, 1928/1933
Gouache with coloured pencil and graphite
over colour monotype on paper
16 x 22.6 cm (6⁵⁄₁₆ x 8⅞ in.)
Gift of Colonel R. S. McLaughlin, 1969.4.28

CLARENCE GAGNON | The *Maria Chapdelaine* Illustrations

Of the birches, aspens, alders and wild cherries scattered upon the slope, October made splashes of many-tinted red and gold. Throughout these weeks the ruddy brown of mosses, the changeless green of fir and cypress, were no more than a background, a setting only for the ravishing colours of those leaves born with the spring, that perish with the autumn.

—*Maria Chapdelaine*, page 120

October, 1928/1933
Oil or oil pastel and watercolour
over graphite on paper
18 x 20.1 cm (7 1/16 x 7 15/16 in.)
Gift of Colonel R. S. McLaughlin, 1969.4.29

CLARENCE GAGNON | The *Maria Chapdelaine* Illustrations

The two men took the double-handed saw and sawed, sawed, sawed from morning till night; it was then the turn of the axes, and the logs were split as their size required.

—*Maria Chapdelaine*, page 121

Laying in Supplies, 1928/1933
Gouache with coloured pencil
over monotype on paper
19.1 x 22.2 cm (7½ x 8¾ in.)
Gift of Colonel R. S. McLaughlin, 1969.4.31

CLARENCE GAGNON | The *Maria Chapdelaine* Illustrations

The moment for laying in wood is also that of the slaughtering. After entrenching against cold comes the defence against hunger. The quarters of pork went into the brine-tub; from a beam in the shed there hung the side of a fat heifer—the other half sold to people in Honfleur—which the cold would keep fresh till spring.

—*Maria Chapdelaine*, pages 121–122

Killing the Pig, 1928/1933
Watercolour and gouache with graphite and
pastel and/or coloured pencil on paper
19.3 x 19.5 cm (7⅝ x 7¹¹⁄₁₆ in.)
Gift of Colonel R. S. McLaughlin, 1969.4.30

CLARENCE GAGNON | The *Maria Chapdelaine* Illustrations

Since the coming of winter they had often talked at the Chapdelaines about the holidays, and now these were drawing near.

"I am wondering whether we shall have any callers on New Year's Day," said Madame Chapdelaine one evening. She went over the list of all relatives and friends able to make the venture. . . . Possibly Wilfrid or Ferdinand might drive from St. Gédéon if the ice on the lake were in good condition."

—*Maria Chapdelaine*, page 126

Winter, 1928/1933
Gouache over colour monotype on paper
17.7 x 24.7 cm (7 x 9¾ in.)
Gift of Colonel R. S. McLaughlin, 1969.4.32

CLARENCE GAGNON | The *Maria Chapdelaine* Illustrations

To go to midnight mass is the natural and strong desire of every French-Canadian peasant, even of those living farthest from the settlements.

—*Maria Chapdelaine*, page 127

Christmas Mass, 1928/1933
Pastel and/or coloured pencil on paper
18.2 x 21.8 cm (7³⁄₁₆ x 8⁹⁄₁₆ in.)
Gift of Colonel R. S. McLaughlin, 1969.4.34

CLARENCE GAGNON | The *Maria Chapdelaine* Illustrations

But towards the middle of December much snow fell, dry and fine as dust, and three days before Christmas the north-west wind arose and made an end of the roads. On the morrow of the storm Chapdelaine harnessed Charles-Eugène to the heavy sleigh and departed with Tit'Bé; they took shovels to clear the way or lay out another route.

—*Maria Chapdelaine*, page 128

The Day After the Storm, 1928/1933
Gouache over colour monotype on paper
18 x 20.5 cm (7 1/16 x 8 1/16 in.)
Gift of Colonel R. S. McLaughlin, 1969.4.33

CLARENCE GAGNON | The *Maria Chapdelaine* Illustrations

Dreaming of his return, of François, the handsome sunburnt face turned to hers, Maria forgets all else, and looks long with unseeing eyes at the snow-covered ground which the moonlight has turned into a glittering extent of some magic texture, like to ivory and mother-of-pearl—at the black pattern of the fences outlined upon it, and the menacing ranks of the dark forest.

—*Maria Chapdelaine*, pages 141–142

Snow-clad Hills, 1928/1933
Oil pastel with gouache on paper
15.9 x 22.9 cm (6¼ x 9 in.)
Gift of Colonel R. S. McLaughlin, 1969.4.35

CLARENCE GAGNON | The *Maria Chapdelaine* Illustrations

"This is what happened. You knew perhaps that he was foreman in a shanty above La Tuque, on the Vermilion River. About the middle of December he suddenly told the boss that he was going off to spend Christmas and New Year at Lake St. John—up here. . . . The boss did not wish him to go and said so plainly; but you know François—a man not to be thwarted when a notion entered his head. He answered that he was set on going to the Lake for the holidays, and that go he would. . . .

"The shanty was not very far in the woods, only two days' journey from the Transcontinental which passes La Tuque."

—*Maria Chapdelaine*, pages 146–147

Logging Camp Near Vermillion, 1928/1933
Gouache with coloured pencil over
colour monotype on paper
18 x 22 cm (7 1/16 x 8 11/16 in.)
Gift of Colonel R. S. McLaughlin, 1969.4.36

CLARENCE GAGNON | The *Maria Chapdelaine* Illustrations

She sees François making his way through the close-set trees, limbs stiffened with the cold, his skin raw with that pitiless nor'wester, gnawed by hunger, stumbling with fatigue, his feet so weary that with no longer strength to lift them his snow-shoes often catch the snow and throw him to his knees.

—*Maria Chapdelaine*, pages 156–157

François Paradis in the Blizzard, 1928/1933
Gouache and watercolour with pastel
and/or coloured pencil on paper
18.8 x 21.7 cm (7⅜ x 8 9/16 in.)
Gift of Colonel R. S. McLaughlin, 1969.4.37

CLARENCE GAGNON | The *Maria Chapdelaine* Illustrations

One evening in February Samuel Chapdelaine said to his daughter: "The roads are passable; if you wish it, Maria, we shall go to La Pipe on Sunday for the mass."

—*Maria Chapdelaine*, page 161

St. Henri de Taillon, 1928/1933
Pastel and/or coloured pencil with graphite,
gouache and watercolour on paper
16 x 23.5 cm (6⁵⁄₁₆ x 9¼ in.)
Gift of Colonel R. S. McLaughlin, 1969.4.38

CLARENCE GAGNON | The *Maria Chapdelaine* Illustrations

They passed through Honfleur, a hamlet of eight scattered houses, and then re-entered the woods. After a time they came upon clearings, then houses appeared dotted along the road; little by little the dusky ranks of the forest retreated, and soon they were in the village with other sleighs before and following them, all going toward the church.

—*Maria Chapdelaine*, page 163

Honfleur, 1928/1933
Gouache over colour monotype on paper
20.5 x 19.9 cm (8 1/16 x 7 13/16 in.)
Gift of Colonel R. S. McLaughlin, 1969.4.39

CLARENCE GAGNON | The *Maria Chapdelaine* Illustrations

March came, and one day Tit'Bé brought the news from Honfleur that there would be a large gathering in the evening at Ephrem Surprenant's to which everyone was invited. . . .

    Honfleur, the nearest village to their house, was eight miles away; but what were eight miles over the snow and through the woods compared with the delight of hearing songs and stories, and of talk with people from afar?

—*Maria Chapdelaine*, page 171

March, 1928/1933
Gouache with pastel and/or
coloured pencil on paper
17.9 x 24.3 cm (7 1/16 x 9 9/16 in.)
Gift of Colonel R. S. McLaughlin, 1969.4.40

CLARENCE GAGNON | The *Maria Chapdelaine* Illustrations

"This . . . this is no place for you, Maria. The country is too rough, the work too hard; merely to earn one's bread is killing toil."

—*Maria Chapdelaine*, page 188

Spring Mud, 1928/1933
Gouache and watercolour
over graphite on paper
20.6 x 19.7 cm (8⅛ x 7¾ in.)
Gift of Colonel R. S. McLaughlin, 1969.4.41

CLARENCE GAGNON | The *Maria Chapdelaine* Illustrations

All of her life had Maria known this cold, this snow, the land's death-like sleep, these austere frowning woods; for the first time now she viewed them with fear and hate. A paradise surely must it be, this country to the south where March is no longer winter and in April the leaves are green! At mid-winter one takes to the road without snow-shoes, unclad in furs, beyond sight of the cruel forest. And the cities . . . the pavements . . .

—*Maria Chapdelaine*, page 191

Preparing the Soil, 1928/1933
Gouache with coloured pencil and graphite
over colour monotype on paper
21 x 20.6 cm (8¼ x 8⅛ in.)
Gift of Colonel R. S. McLaughlin, 1969.4.42

CLARENCE GAGNON | The *Maria Chapdelaine* Illustrations

François had come in the full tide of summer, from the land of mystery at the head-waters of the rivers; the memory of his artless words brought back the dazzling sunshine, the ripened blueberries and the last blossoms of the laurel fading in the undergrowth.

—*Maria Chapdelaine*, page 194

Hills at Dusk, 1928/1933
Gouache with coloured pencil over
colour monotype on paper
16.2 x 21.9 cm (6⅜ x 8⅝ in.)
Gift of Colonel R. S. McLaughlin, 1969.4.43

CLARENCE GAGNON | The *Maria Chapdelaine* Illustrations

Close and ill-smelling, the floor littered with manure and foul straw, the pump in one corner that was so hard to work and set the teeth on edge with its grinding; the weather-beaten outside; buffeted by wind and never-ending snow—sign and symbol of what awaited her were she to marry one like Eutrope Gagnon, and accept as her lot a lifetime of rude toil in this sad and desolate land . . .

—*Maria Chapdelaine*, page 200

Fetching Water, 1928/1933
Oil pastel over graphite on paper
20.4 x 19.8 cm (8 1/16 x 7 13/16 in.)
Gift of Colonel R. S. McLaughlin, 1969.4.44

CLARENCE GAGNON | The *Maria Chapdelaine* Illustrations

That cruel north-west wind that heaped the snow above François Paradis at the foot of some desolate cypress, bore also to her on its wings the frown and the harshness of the country wherein she dwelt, and filled her with hate of the northern winter, the cold, the whitened ground and the loneliness, of those measureless woods concerned not with the destinies of men, where every melancholy tree is fit to stand in a home of the dead.

—*Maria Chapdelaine*, pages 204–205

April, 1928/1933
Gouache over colour monotype on paper
20.7 x 26.6 cm (8⅛ x 10½ in.)
Gift of Colonel R. S. McLaughlin, 1969.4.45

CLARENCE GAGNON | The *Maria Chapdelaine* Illustrations

Her eyes open in the ghostly dawn, Maria gave ear to the sounds of his departure: the banging of the stable door against the wall; the horse's hoofs thudding on the wood of the alley; muffled commands to Charles-Eugène: "Hold up, there! Back . . . Back up! Whoa!" Then the tinkle of the sleigh-bells. In the silence that followed, the sick woman groaned two or three times in her sleep; Maria watched the wan light stealing into the house and thought of her father's journey, trying to reckon up the distances he must travel.

—*Maria Chapdelaine*, pages 213–214

Going for the Doctor, 1928/1933
Gouache over colour monotype on paper
18.1 x 19.8 cm (7⅛ x 7¹³⁄₁₆ in.)
Gift of Colonel R. S. McLaughlin, 1969.4.46

CLARENCE GAGNON | The *Maria Chapdelaine* Illustrations

Then there was apparently nothing more to be done; the men lit their pipes, and the doctor, with his feet against the stove, held forth as to his professional labours and the cures he had wrought.

—*Maria Chapdelaine*, page 219

The Diagnosis, 1928/1933
Pastel and/or coloured pencil
over graphite on paper
19.7 x 22.5 cm (7¾ x 8⅞ in.)
Gift of Colonel R. S. McLaughlin, 1969.4.47

CLARENCE GAGNON | The *Maria Chapdelaine* Illustrations

About midnight came Eutrope Gagnon, bringing Tit'Sèbe the bone-setter. He was a little, thin, sad-faced man with very kind eyes. As always when called to a sick-bed, he wore his clothes of ceremony, of dark well-worn cloth, which he bore with the awkwardness of the peasant in Sunday attire.

—*Maria Chapdelaine*, page 227

At the Sickbed, 1928/1933
Gouache with coloured pencil over
colour monotype on paper
19.7 x 21.7 cm (7¾ x 8 9/16 in.)
Gift of Colonel R. S. McLaughlin, 1969.4.48

CLARENCE GAGNON | The *Maria Chapdelaine* Illustrations

While the priest performed the sacred rites, and his low words mingled with the sighs of the dying woman, Samuel Chapdelaine and his children were praying with bended heads; in some sort consoled, released from anxiousness and doubt, confident that a sure pact was then concluding with the Almighty for the blue skies of Paradise spangled with stars of gold as a rightful heritage.

—*Maria Chapdelaine*, page 235

Last Rites, 1928/1933
Oil pastel with gouache on paper
19.8 x 20.4 cm (7$^{13}/_{16}$ x 8$^{1}/_{16}$ in.)
Gift of Colonel R. S. McLaughlin, 1969.4.49

CLARENCE GAGNON | The *Maria Chapdelaine* Illustrations

Towards four o'clock the wind leaped to the south-east, and the storm ended swiftly as a wave that sinks broken from the shore; in the strange deep silence after the tumult the mother sighed, sighed once again, and died.

—*Maria Chapdelaine*, page 235

Dawn, 1928/1933
Gouache and oil pastel with
watercolour on paper
17.3 x 26.2 cm (6 13/16 x 10 5/16 in.)
Gift of Colonel R. S. McLaughlin, 1969.4.50

CLARENCE GAGNON | The *Maria Chapdelaine* Illustrations

A long silence followed, in which Samuel Chapdelaine's head nodded slowly towards his breast and it seemed as though he were falling asleep. Maria spoke quickly to him, in fear of his offending:—"Father! Do not sleep!"

—*Maria Chapdelaine*, page 239

A Lonely House, 1928/1933
Gouache with coloured pencil over
colour monotype on paper
19.5 x 19.6 cm (7 11/16 x 7 11/16 in.)
Gift of Colonel R. S. McLaughlin, 1969.4.53

CLARENCE GAGNON | The *Maria Chapdelaine* Illustrations

"But your mother snatched a stick from the ground and made straight for the bears, screaming at them:—'Our beautiful fat sheep! Be off with you, you ugly thieves, or I will do for you!' I got there at my best speed, leaping over the stumps; but by that time the bears had cleared off into the woods without showing fight, scared as could be, because she had put the fear of death into them."

—*Maria Chapdelaine*, page 244

Protecting the Flock, 1928/1933
Gouache over colour monotype on paper
21.4 x 21.4 cm (8 7/16 x 8 7/16 in.)
Gift of Colonel R. S. McLaughlin, 1969.4.52

CLARENCE GAGNON | The *Maria Chapdelaine* Illustrations

To strive from dawn till nightfall, spending all her strength in a thousand heavy tasks, and yet from dawn till nightfall never losing patience nor her happy tranquillity; continually to see about her only the wilderness, the great pitiless forest, and to hold in the midst of it all an ordered way of life, the gentleness and the joyousness which are the fruits of many a century sheltered from such rudeness—was it not surely a hard thing and a worthy? And the recompense? After death, a little word of praise.

—*Maria Chapdelaine*, page 250

Sugaring, 1928/1933
Pastel and/or coloured pencil
with gouache on paper
22.1 x 22.5 cm (8 11/16 x 8 7/8 in.)
Gift of Colonel R. S. McLaughlin, 1969.4.51

CLARENCE GAGNON | The *Maria Chapdelaine* Illustrations

And Maria answered him:—"Yes . . . If you wish I will marry you as you asked me to—the spring after this spring now—when the men come back from the woods for the sowing."

—*Maria Chapdelaine*, page 263

The Betrothal, 1928/1933
Gouache over colour monotype on paper
21.5 x 22.6 cm (8⁷⁄₁₆ x 8⅞ in.)
Gift of Colonel R. S. McLaughlin, 1969.4.54

About the Author

Ian M. Thom is a distinguished art historian and curator with more than forty years of art museum experience. He has held senior curatorial positions at the Vancouver Art Gallery, the Art Gallery of Greater Victoria and the McMichael Canadian Art Collection. The author of numerous books and catalogues, he was made a member of the Order of Canada in 2009.